UNMUTED

❧

DAVID ANDREW TITTLE

unmuted

This book is a long overdue love letter to myself:

"Never forget your pain has brought you beauty and that your
happiness is healthy—
That your words deserve to be heard—
That your thoughts, so long silent, can shine with light and power—
Sing your songs, shout your verses, let your voice ring out with
confidence and clarity—

I am proud of me."

CONTENTS

FOREWORD

It is probably poor form to preface a book of poems with a poem, especially a book as good as this one—(*you'll see!*)—and yet, I'm finding prose unfit to the sacred task I've been given.

Since childhood, poetry has been a shared language with my brother. Our father turned to it—astutely—to impart insights and feelings he hoped would guide us despite struggles to voice them himself; our mother—faithfully, lovingly, steadfastly—wove it into the fabric of our home through song; and we—independently—learned to set to verse all we hesitated to say but still longed to acknowledge. Over the years, poems have been the letters we've written each other —ways we've reached out to each other—comforted each other— learned each other. So, when David asked me to introduce his poetry to you, a poem, even if inappropriate—*especially* if inappropriate—was the only thing .

these were not
    written for either of us
    and somehow, finding us now
    have become ours

these are incantations
    that created have recreated their maker
    ever more powerfully
    in his OWN image

these are guides
    maps to difficult lands
    some treacherous in their anger and grief
    some hopeful and therefore all the more so

these are a gift
    long awaited
    but never offered
    until they could be freely given

these are only the beginning and
    that
    is what I love best of all

The book you're holding in front of you is by my favorite poet—and when he told me he was writing it, I made the joke we should title it *"About Fucking Time!"*

In all honesty, it would be more accurate to say this is FINALLY the right time.

I'm so excited for you that you have this in your hands!

— Lisa Tittle Caballero

PREFACE

I have always had a complicated affair with words.

My parents introduced a love of literature and poetry early. I was easily enamored by the way words could be strung together to pull me into other realms and realities, and was soon attempting to use them to create magic of my own. Growing up bilingual, I had the luxury of an "extra" vocabulary to pull from—and my hometown of Calexico was a perfect place to practice weaving the best words of each into the Spanglish cultural collage de la frontera. Words were the fuel that powered the engine of my childhood—the knowledge, imagination, music, humor, romance, and dreams.

But words were weapons, too—incendiary devices which, when tossed into the powder kegs of location, tensions and circumstance, could do devastating damage—and a byproduct of my biracial upbringing was I was a frequent target of the full force *all* those words could apply. By necessity, I learned language as a deployable defense, and retaliated by honing it as (*sometimes deplorable*) offense. The violence of those early verbal exchanges was breathtaking—the precision and fury of the thrusts, parries and counterattacks made it impossible to escape unscathed—even when victorious—and left me

PREFACE

convinced whoever wrote the "sticks and stones" adage had never experienced the Calecia concept of carrilla.

In this complicated confluence of influences and expressions, words were both poison and antidote. I was often found scribbling salves for the wounds they inflicted, or writing myself into worlds where I was, if not heroic, then at least conveniently invisible. Even after I left—ricocheting from West Coast to East Coast and back—Calexico to Yale to LA—culture to culture to culture—I carried this convenient cloak of private communication with me; a security blanket to comfort and cover me in all the places I felt unseen, unknown, or unwelcome—my own head, included. I wrote myself safety nets, triumphant odes, angry screeds and love notes—then tucked them away in notebooks and binders—externalized memories and reminders of where I'd been—*who* I'd been.

They were never intended to be shared—at least not beyond the limited scope of those with the dubious privilege of membership in my private poetry circle. In my most daring dreams, I imagined them discovered *post mortem* and shared with a selective few—future historical relics in the same vein as the love letters my father wrote to my mother during my childhood.

But something has changed—in me—in the world—in the way we, as a society, are talking to each other—the way we're talking *about* each other. Those of us who have learned, through love and pain, to respect, cherish and *balance* the power of words—as both bane and balm—have been drowned out by the sewage of sounds employed by people with malevolent aims and twisted intent.

So I do not see it as mere coincidence that it is—at *precisely* this moment of historic inflection—my own spiritual evolution and maturation has caused my private thoughts and words to morph from safety blanket to a mantle *demanding* to be seen and heard.

Let me be, abundantly, clear: not all my words are angry, even when employed in service of righteous indignation. Not all of them are healthy—having been written in, and from, places meant to be passed through, not settled in. I even suffer from enough humility and self-awareness to know not all of them are good (*obviously, I like them well enough but, if nothing else, am willing to concede not everyone shares my love of a well-placed F bomb).* My decision to suddenly share some of them is less a claim to quality or value, and more a realization of the need for *solidarity.*

I have a sincere desire for people to enjoy my words. And, truly, I believe they are worth enjoying. I send them into the world with a prayer that even *one* of my poems will touch someone in a way that positively alters the course of their life. I believe they are capable of that. But, the truest power of my words is already realized by adding my voice to a growing swell of others choosing peace, edification, inclusion, spiritual elevation, righteous anger, legitimate protest *(peaceful or otherwise)* in defiance of malicious ideals and, above all, real love.

When viewed in that context, the words I say matter less than the intentions with which I say them—and much less than the voices I, potentially, empower with my support. With this book, I pour my drops into the rising tide of our higher consciousness—and, allowing myself the conceit of quoting myself, close with an invitation:

"I am here
    Now. Come find me."

—David Andrew Tittle

UNMUTED

by
DAVID ANDREW TITTLE

INTRODUCTION

This is not a book for the well-behaved.

These poems were written in the margins—of polite conversation, of institutional forms, of the neat little boxes we're expected to check without protest. They are notes scrawled in the back row, confessions whispered in private, and truths I could not carry any longer without setting them down.

Unmuted was born out of necessity. Not as a performance, but as resistance. As reclamation. As a record. Because silence—particularly the kind imposed on the marginalized, the inconvenient, the "too much"—is not neutral. It's compliance. And I was never very good at that.

This collection draws on a lifetime of asking the "wrong" questions out loud. Of naming what others hoped would go unspoken. Of peeling back the layers—racial, cultural, familial, personal—to see what truths were hiding underneath the palatable surface. You'll find no tidy resolutions here. No reverence for institutions that have not earned it. But you will find teeth. And tenderness. And a refusal to go quietly.

Each section cracks open a different door. Some lead to memory. Some to rage. Some to identity so complicated it can't be mapped without metaphor. But they all lead toward something truer than what we're told to accept.

These are not just poems. They're blueprints. Warnings. Mirrors. Megaphones. And sometimes, maybe, a way home.

So read them out loud if you must. Whisper them if you can't. Just don't look away.

BLUEPRINTS & BARRIERS

"The world is before you and you need not take it or leave it as it was when you came in."
— James Baldwin

Where everything begins: birth, behavior, and the invisible systems that shape us before we know our own names.

FIRST

What was I
    First?

A name?

A thought
    In a little boy's mind,
    When he dreamt
    Of what kind
    Of life he'd live?
    What kind of life
    He'd give to a son
    Or a daughter?

Did I start as ideas
    Soldered together
    From heart and hope?
    Or was the scope
    Of my beginning

Darker—wider—broader?

Was I the dream
    Of another man's daughter,
    Finding herself
    Bound by expectations
    She felt powerless
    To resist?
    Less
    A revelation
    And more
    A function of this
    Mandatory limitation
    Placed on future?

Was I
    Nurture, not Nature?

Was I
    By Choice? Or by
    Voice silenced
    In the face
    Of the unfailing
    Hold of roles
    Defined by patriarchy?

What is me?
    Why is me?

(*Woe is me?*)

I can't *unsee*
    Potential lines
    That led to me—

The way that history
Pointed me towards
Gender engendered
(*Unnaturally?*).

But what if
What was first
Was *me*? Before
I ever *came* to be,
What if
I just *was*, easily?

What if
Power,
Light
And sound
Gathered round
And let me be
Whatever I might
Choose to be?

What if,
Before the world
Could get to me—
Before I could forget
To be—
I had it all
And set it free?

Let's think this thought,
Just for fun—
What if
I am everyone?

If I am
 They
 And *they* is me,
 This all plays out
 So differently.
 We'd cease to be
 A point in time
 (*If mine was yours*
 And yours was mine)—

This paradigm
 Would shift, you see
 And be
 More like a rhythm—
 A rhyme recited,
 Flawlessly.
 Less *me*—
 More *we*—
 And all the lines
 That led to me
 Would simply be
 Our poetry.

I could not judge
 And be not judged,
 With bias grounded
 Biblically
 (*If I was they*
 And they was me)—

I know I say this
 Whimsically—
 But if I was all
 And set it free, then

All I ever have to be
Is *worthy*—

And it will all come back

To me.

DR. FRANKENSTEIN

It was not enough
   To be potential
   I was born with—
   Had to be
   Someone *important*
   Or all this talent
   Would be misspent
   Youth spent chasing
   Truths I could never reach—

Cuz they were not me
   Not mine
   Not fine
   Not even a real line
   Of thought—just a web of
   Your own lies
   I got caught up in

Logic you injected me with—
   Shit you made up

And infected me with—
Ideals you expected me
To respect you with
While you neglected me
With good intentions—
And condescension
For lack of comprehension
Or any (*innocent!*) dissension
From accepted means
Of vying for attention
Or approval

I could remove all
Hope of any empathy
For me or run the risk
That I would
Selfishly
Expect too much of you
For me and fail to see
The bigger picture
Only you saw

Clearly—

Before you even met me
You made me
Resemble
All the parts of you
Passed on to me
And randomly assembled into
Memories I have
To remake and dissemble
So they don't
Resemble monstrosities—

Recycling grace and pride
    You freely gave
    The world outside but
    Intentionally
    Tried to keep from me

You knew
    What it would mean
    To me

To be seen
    To be heard
    Just to hear
    Those fucking words—
    Not assumed
    Not inferred
    Not ideologically deterred
    From being a beast
    Getting less than the least
    You would give a stranger

You knew the danger
    It would raise to me
    For all my praise to be
    Not yours
    But theirs and mine—
    To leave me
    Piecing my ego together
    Like some fucking Frankenstein's
    Monster of feelings—
    To send me
    Reeling with rejection
    Into my mind—

The one constantly

Trying to *end* me

The one you bragged
   You gave me

But you didn't try
   To save me

Yet here I am
   Still hoping
   I can find some resolution
   Still coping
   With this minor chord
   Played on the ties that bind me
   To this entirely
   Avoidable conclusion

That

While much of you
   Was heaven sent
   For others—
   My mother
   My sister
   My brothers
   My sense of me
   My sense of dignity
   My self-respect—
   Were all apparently
   Just some fucking experiment
   On how not to be
   A parent

I am
   Inherently

Part of you
And you of me
And I will never be
Free from the identity
You forced on me
When you flipped the switch
On all the parts you stitched
So carefully

But I will find the way
To make this bloodline
Mine
To *take* the name
You sewed on me
This history
Bestowed on me—

To be my own creature—

To feature my *self*
More prominently
To be my Shelley
To your Frankenstein

To take the time
To self-reflect
And piece these
Gory aspects together
Into my own story

'Cause whether
I am good
Or not
This life is all
The me I've got

So I will take the knife
    To me—excise these doubts
    These insecurities
    And without you
    But *truly* me—
    Be well
    And truly

Proud of me.

TRIBULATION

I have been
    To the bottom,
    Face down in the place
    Found only in spaces
    That should be
    Beneath our feet—

Where we meet
    The versions of ourselves
    We tell ourselves
    We will never be—
    Could never be.

I have been
    To the abyss—
    So deep
    No one would miss me
    If I stayed
    In the far below—afraid
    No one would even know

I was gone.

I have seen dawn break,
    Dark and bleak,
    Finding me
    Meek before my demons
    And ghosts—
    Where the most
    I could do was lie
    To my hosts of fears
    About why I would not stay
    Here.

I have been
    Broken and scared—
    Impaired, lonely and abandoned—

Have stuck my hand in the fire
    And called my pain
    A liar, for all the ways
    It's tried to guide me
    To safety.

I have not always thrived,
    But I have *always* survived.

And I have been
    Free, too. You've seen it,
    (I hope)
    The way I flit away
    From the punch—
    The hit—the bad day.

These things have a scope
    I have learned

To manage—
To salvage—
To leverage into strength
And wisdom—

So I can become
A better ruler
Over the kingdom
Of my thoughts.

I have bought myself
Time for my evolution—
Quelled revolutions
In my mind—allowed myself
To find me
Being happy, sooner—
Faster!

This banshee?
I will outlast her.
This ogre will not best me.
Beasts and barriers
Will not arrest me
On my journey to
The best me.

I have been here before—

Fucking test me.

SATURDAY MOURNING

Laying in bed,
    I could hear Handel
    Playing on the HiFi.

Before I even opened
    My eyes, I could smell
    The scents of corned beef hash
    Or pancakes—the secret recipe
    Designed to wake me
    From my slumber.

I'd lumber to the kitchen
    To see if there was coffee,
    And find Daddy
    Where I knew he'd be—

In the kitchen
    By the stove, frying
    And flipping a treasure trove
    Of flavor and memory.

I knew there'd be more
    To it than breakfast—
    There would be questions—
    Debates about how late
    Was too late to wake up—
    And chores in store,
    After I ate—

But sitting there
    With a full plate,
    I knew the tasks would wait
    Till he was done
    Feeding me.

In these moments,
    Preceding mowing
    And clipping branches,
    I could feel time
    Slipping forward—growing
    Bones strengthening—
    My time with him
    Lengthening into permanence—

Into remembrance.

Those mornings with him
    Were an extravagance—
    Every second spent with me,
    Less time he had for others.

There would be more
    Time for me
    (*If I'd had my druthers*)—
    But living with a man
    Who cared (*so passionately!*)

For his world and
Legacy had its cost.

Still, on those mornings
   Filled with pancakes
   And conversation
   Casually tossed
   Into my childhood—

Life was good.

I would do it again
   (If I could)—
   Sit at that table
   And fill my plate
   With all the moments
   I was able to fit
   In time and space.

I would listen—
   Stuff my face with memories
   Until my heart
   Could take no more.

I would even do chores.

THE CAST IRON PAN

There was a cast iron pan
    In the cupboard. I remembered
    To take it with me
    When I left.

There were other memories
    Of my mother
    I had to leave
    Behind—

A closet full of blouses
    Was donated to the hope
    They would, someday, hang
    In other people's houses—

Empty frames and board games—
    Some with names
    On sticky notes stuck
    To them, as if a bargain
    Had been struck by a buyer

For the past.

That cast iron pan
    Was unnamed, though—
    An unclaimed history
    Of the ground beef and beans
    That had sustained me
    Through my childhood and teens—

Sustenance, seasoned with oregano
    And the love of the mother I know
    Was living within her means, but beyond
    Her skill set. I had my own,
    But I could not let it lie,

Unwanted. I said goodbye
    To her house—
    But the pan came with me,

To be used in the culinary arts
    That had skipped a generation,
    And to preserve a fullness of heart
    Which had not. Now it sits
    In my kitchen, and serves
    As an ironclad reminder—

My mom was not a cook—
    But every time I look at that pan,
    I understand—

I remember.

She fed me well.

OPENING DOORS

I was raised
    In the warmth
    Of good behavior,
    With a frosty edge
    Of *"good fences make good neighbors."*

Where etiquette, once
    Universally praised as the savior
    Of societal ills, was still valued
    And expected.

Where people did not take
    Kindly to being disrespected.

Where those on the margins
    Were meant to receive
    These gestures as
    (Admittedly inadequate) compensation
    For the ways society, historically,
    Asked we stay in narrow lanes—

Designed to diminish
The fact the ways we act
Masked a failure to evolve

More fully. We were taught
These rules and boundaries
Bought us space to ignore
How someone could have more
Than one place—

Not just
The one assigned
At birth and enforced
By gender, inequality
And the color of their face.

Mandatory generosity
Was as much a way
Of keeping me at arm's length,
As it was a means of welcome
And acceptance. Traditions—
Regulated by expectations—
Were, at once, a comfort
And complications
Of the subordination of entire subsets
Of society and creed—

Symbols of the need we felt
To be better than the limitations
Imposed by rule of law,
Written or unspoken.

I recognize these contradictory
Functions of familiar habits—

And though I may have woken
    To a better way,
    It would be a lie
    To say I do not feel
    There is still value—today—
    In treating you like a queen.
    In making you feel seen
    As part of *my* nobility—
    Apart from me—
    But the highest ranking part of me
    And my personal society.

At best, these fences
    And borders are built around me
    So things can appear
    To function properly. Civilly.
    But, more importantly,
    I find they exist (*necessarily!*)
    So you can see me

Take them down

For you to more freely
    Enter territories created
    For my safety—

So that when we melt
    Into each other
    You can clearly feel
    You are no longer *other*—
    That *me* has given way to *we*—
    And my security has been
    (*Willingly and lovingly*)
    Compromised by your existence.

The essence of these habits,
 Born in antiquity,
 Are as much an essential
 Part of me as you are. But
 (Together)
 We are as far
 From their origins
 Of negativity
 As two people
 Have any right to be.

And that's fucking fine
 By me.

GEOMETRY

Lines. Angles. Shapes
    Drawn on graph paper
    With a ruler to keep
    Things straight—protractor
    Working late
    Cause the work was due
    Tomorrow,
    And tomorrow,
    And tomorrow—
    The petty pace creeping on—
    Keeping me on track
    To stay in my place,

Tracing lines, angles
    And shapes—triangulating
    My societal position
    With mathematical
    Precision—surgically
    Shallow incisions
    With lead tips

On processed wood—
Showing my work
To prove I understood
The assignment—
Reinforcing my alignment
With time spent

Standing in lines—
Ingesting angles—
My life taking shape
According to theorems,
And stratagems devised
By them.

Then, I
Gradually graduated
From cosines and gradients
With perfect grades
And accolades awarded
As if they were signs
Of future success—
When, in truth,
They were merely proof
I had misplayed my youth

Believing lines and angles—
Fabricated shapes,
Predicated on the fear
I might *(someday)* be
More awake—anticipating
Potential mental rebellions
And castrating them
By forcing me to dedicate
My brain to playing games
That were rigged

From the start.

I committed to the part—
    Reading my lines
    And learning my angles
    While the stage took shape,
    And the rulers
    Kept the cast confined
    In the straight
    And narrow columns
    They'd constructed.

But now I want
    To deconstruct
    All of it—every line,
    Angle and shape
    Should be mine—
    My intelligence and power
    Redefined
    By something sacred—

A Fibonacci sequence
    Spiraling outward
    From inside my head,
    Diverging gracefully
    From the lies
    I've been fed
    About who I am
    And what I can
    And cannot do—
    Leading to truths,
    Self generated,
    Validated and venerated
    By *me*. Now,

I am awake, again.
    I see a way to be
    Free from my programming—
    A path to autonomy—
    From the rules and regulations
    That have limited
    My imagination to things
    Someone *else* thought up.

And, when I am no longer
    Caught up in the quiet traps
    Of society I can,
    Finally, be free
    To be unfinished and raw.
    To draw my own lines—
    Create my own angles—
    Escape this altered reality—

And let the *real* me
    Take shape.

UNLEARNED

It was a lesson,
    Perhaps learned before
    My consciousness
    Had even turned on—

A foregone conclusion
    Reached before anyone
    Had a chance to teach me

Anything. Inherited,
    (My mother would say)
    This way I—unlike others—
    Spurn happiness and hope,
    Lest losing them
    Inflict more misery on me
    Than the pain and sadness
    Of being without.

Again and again

This trope has been
Reinforced beyond doubt—
By history, and the dark
Part of me I am
Loathe to be free of.

Ever the misanthrope,
I love not so I lose not—
And the perceived plot
Against me grows in scope
And power—strengthened
By each joyless hour,
Day and year
It is allowed to exist—
Until I fear this
Is, simply, my identity.

But does it have to be?

Have I no agency
In correcting the dread
I am used
To expecting?
Can't I, instead,
Choose differently?

Perhaps this thing I see
As a curse to suffer
Stoically, is simply
A correctable inability
To be heroically
(*Stupidly!*)
Happy.

We shall see,
    My friends—

We shall see.

BORDERS, BURDENS &
BELONGING

"It is not our differences that divide us. It is our inability to recognize, accept, and celebrate those differences."
— Audre Lorde

Family stories, fractured roots, and the borders—seen and unseen—that define where we come from, how we speak, and where we are allowed to stand.

COMPLEX COMPLEXION

I am half
    As brown as him.
    My name gives me away—
    Or is it my reflection
    In his stereotype?

I am
    Something less than ethnic.
    It seems
    To be the consensus.

I am
    (Who?)
    Popular opinion.

I am
    Certain he sees the other me—
    The me I see
    In most of America *(at least*
    The one I live in

Now). I am judged
By my own
Opinions.

"White is white—
   Nothing
   But the insult at the end of my name,"
Right? But am I

(Careful!)

White?

I am
   Sorry for forgetting who
   I am

In his eyes. At least

Half of me resents the other for being
   Obvious.

I envy his skin color.
   He comments on mine.

Does that make one of us

Racist?

CASTING STONES

On summer days in the California desert,
    The winds chase the devil
    In the dust away from the sunset,
    And toward the halos of barbed wire
    That scar the earth—and mark the distance
    Between two worlds.

When I was a kid, my best friend lived
    In the projects by *"the fence."* In the afternoon,
    We'd dance in the automatic sprinklers—
    Chasing the sleeping lizards from their spots
    On the cinderblocks and scaring the cicadas.

But when it was too hot *(even for the lizards),*
    We'd hide, snickering, in the shade
    Of the backyard wall—
    And throw rocks at the Mexicans
    As they perched on the fence.

Whenever we'd hit one, we'd laugh—the tears

Parting the dirt on our faces—leaving
Streaks of wet through the brown.
Then, smothering giggles, we'd scrabble
For more ammunition.

The men would curse us,
Saying all the Spanish words we knew
We shouldn't know—but what could they do?

They were on the wrong side of the border
And we were American.

So we'd bury our hands
(*his brown, mine white*)
In the fertile soil, lending dust to the wind
As we hunted for more stones to throw.

Later that summer, la migra
Shot a fourteen year old *"mojado"* in the back
As he sat on the fence—

They said he had a rock in his hand.

31 FLAVORS

I'd see the signs
    But know we couldn't go—
    Most of the time.

And, most of the time,
    That was fine. We were
    Poor, and wanting more
    Was a rich kid's scene.

We had 3 day bread
    And (*sometimes*) Ovaltine
    At home, that I could eat
    And drink while sweet things
    Roamed my head
    In drive-by dreams
    Of cookies and cream.

Rocky roads were truths,
    Not treats, most days—
    But we coped.

Still, the scope of my innocent hopes
    Was measured in two scoops
    And fudge—sprinkled with faith
    And fantasies looped around
    Belief, unbudging,
    That life was fair—
    That there was enough
    For all—that when
    Everyone else had
    Had their fill of 31
    And fate finally favored me,
    There would still be
    One flavor left for me.

And most days—
    Most of the time—
    That was fine.

But there were days
    And times, when the line
    Between truth
    And the naïveté of destitute youth
    Was blurred—when my
    Hopes, unheard, incurred
    The wrath of resentment.
    When money spent, meant
    Necessities, not niceties—
    And envy got the best of me.

Why were caramel swirls
    And mint chocolate chips
    Skipping me, not them?
    When was my turn
    In that magical line
    Of sweet destiny?

Those days—
    Those times—
    I was not fine.

I wanted theirs,
    And *also* mine.
    My cookie dough—
    Their ice cream cake—
    To take the things
    I'd always lacked
    And drizzle them
    With sweet payback
    For all the times
    I, childishly,
    Chose *happy*
    Over *gluttony.*

Now I have lots.
    So, I forget *(sometimes)*
    Those had nots—
    Those times of *I wants*
    And *they gots*
    That taught a little boy
    To want lots—
    To fight the fear of neediness
    By chasing *stuff,*
    Not happiness.

I still see signs
    Of the boy who couldn't go.
    Most of the time,
    He is fine
    Without the sugar rush.

He is tough and wise

Beyond his years. And I,
Getting up in mine—
With ice cream on demand—
With *all* the flavors close at hand—
Am proud of his restraint.
How he goes without,
Without bitterness or complaint.

Most days.
    Most of the time.

I forget *(sometimes)*
    His pain is mine.
    That he had it rough.
    That his life felt unkind.
    That unless *I* hug him
    And tell him he's fine—

Even 31 flavors
    Is not enough.

TIRANDO FIESTA

Carne asadas
　　Never start on time.

You might think
　　It's fine to show up
　　At three
　　(After all that's when
　　The thing is
　　Supposed to be),
　　But all you see
　　When you get there
　　Are awkward stares—
　　Someone's nana
　　Still fixing her hair—
　　And then you end up helping
　　With mesas and chairs.

Unwritten rules
　　We grew up with—

Like show up with beers
For the compas
You threw up with
That one night
We stayed up
With Cente and tears—
Cahuamas y carcajadas—
Pinches mamadas—
Secretos sagrados
We *needed* to hear:

Dolores—angustias—
    The fears we all carried, quietly—
    Carrilla que *(en serio!)*
    Se pasaba de lanza—
    Las tranzas y traiciones—
    Nuestras malas decisiones—
    The ways we felt,
    But could never say
    At least not without a
    "¡No te aguites, güey!"

But that night
    Y otras iguales
    We talked about love—
    Familia—el jale—
    We swore at each other,
    But swore to each other
    (Sea lo que sea)
    We would always be
    Brothers—

And nothing else mattered.

Then life scattered us—
    Bruised and battered us—
    Tore and shattered us.
    Trust was abused.
    We, sometimes,
    Used the wrong words
    To try to make it right—
    Started friendship-ending
    Fights por tercos—
    Por pendejos.

We got older
    And forgot those shoulders
    We relied on—
    Leaned on—
    Cried on—
    Until we believed
    Those days were
    Bygone.

But, even though
    We were estranged,
    Those unwritten rules
    Never changed:

No place is too far
    If you know the way
    Home.
    Si tienes hermanos,
    You are never alone.
    Sometimes putazos
    Son fuertes abrazos.
    And you can never be late
    If you show up

DAVID ANDREW TITTLE

(cuando estés listo)

Con pisto.

REAL TALK

I was born with great privilege
    Borne on the circumstances
    Created by a union
    Still considered sacrilege,
    By some—who cannot see
    Me as both sides of one
    Coin—flipped or spun—
    Mixed race—so, no matter
    Which face ends up
    Showing up at the end
    Of whatever game is played,
    My name still gives me access
    To the safe side
    Of the conversation.

At the slightest foreboding,
    The coding switches
    To the me more likely
    To fit the vibe.

But which *is* the real me?

I've tried to be one
    Or the other, exclusively—
    But, inside, the other side
    Has always felt denied—
    Lied to and marginalized
    By whichever part
    Has more pride of ownership
    At the time.

It feels almost natural—
    The rhyme, rhythm and reason
    With which I match
    Each season of discontent
    With carefully curated
    Characteristics, content,
    Percentages and statistics.

Depending on which sticks
    And stones are being thrown,
    I can own Taino, generic Latino
    Or white hick roots—
    And still feel alone
    When the teams pick players.

Too many layers
    To keep me from making it
    Too deep for casual convo—
    Cuando preguntan
    "Where you from?"
    And *"How come*
    You don't look like no one
    I know?"

¡Que privilegio!
    Mirándome en el espejo
    Con la cara de gabacho—
    Knowing I can go anywhere,
    And the only ones
    Who won't stare
    Are the ones I *least* relate to—
    The ones who might hate to
    Know my *"you"* is equal part *"tu"*—
    Y yo no sabiendo quién soy
    Tampoco, tampers
    With my mental locomotion.

How do I get de aquí to there
    Without explaining
    I have curly hair
    When it's longer—
    And mi papa era gringo
    But my mom was Puerto Rican—
    And I was born en la frontera,
    So I can check esa caja, too?

Como quisiera ser sencillo—
    But even that word
    Tiene doble sentido.
    So, only people like me
    Know that I'm explaining
    Why, even though I shouldn't
    Be complaining about why
    I'm even explaining mi historia—
    Es necesario—so wherever
    I go, puedo pasar
    Tranquilamente

Con la gente

That barely claim me
After I prove I am
One of whatever *"we"*
Me combine.

No pertenezco.

Pero que suerte
Que mi disimulación—
And dissimilation—
Allows me to experience
Discrimination
Wherever I go.

But only I know.

IMMIGRATION

The white bus with blue stripes leaves me
    At the gate—cobblestones and gothic gray
    Welcome me to an unfamiliar future. I waver
    On the sidewalk, swaying
    As other students push past me
    Into their surroundings. Already,
    I miss the brown
    Sounds of the desert—the easy space
    Of one story buildings and front porches—
    Two way streets and fences

I can cross easily.

I feel a sudden loss
    Of breath weaken my shoulders
    And I lower my luggage to the ground.
    I am weightless—rootless—
    Disconnected from the things I've carried
    With me, I can see myself turning
    Into the space around me—

Embracing it with my empty hands—
Cradling prospective dreams in a mind rocked
By the change in scenery. Disoriented,
I realize I've left everything I own
Sitting unguarded on a sidewalk.

I can hear my mother's last minute warnings
Pounding in my forehead—
"Cuidado, mijo.
Don't leave your bags
Lying around in the city"—

And I am ashamed.

Distrustful of the strange faces
Invading my space, I snatch my baggage
From their stares, clutch it to my breast
And, head held high
With false security, I set out
To find the keys

To my new home.

TOO MANY STORIES

There were no two story buildings
    Where I grew up. Well,
    Maybe one. Or two.
    But not a few. Boring?
    Perhaps. But there was always
    A view of the sky.

If you really tried
    (Or hid inside),
    You could miss a sunset.
    But, most days, you'd get
    Purple-blue-orange-pink glory,

Easily. I think

Things were clearer
    When everyone only had one story.

REMEMBRANCE

A thousand lives ago, I was
    Already a steady force
    In the world. Before
    The lines of time had curled
    Around themselves,
    I had found myself—
    Made myself
    A future full of wonder
    Spent on enlightenment,
    Then torn asunder
    And forgotten.

Reborn, repeatedly,
    Each life since
    Has been progressively
    Less whole—more rotten—
    Fruits born of doubt—
    Misbegotten missions
    Without direction or hope.

Still, the scope of time
    Has expanded constantly
    And, finally, landed me
    Here—trying
    To free my head—

To weave threads
    Of history
    Into a tapestry
    Of the best of me,
    And leave the rest of me
    Behind—

To edit the past
    And future me's
    Into a story
    Worthy of the present me—
    With glory (*and humility*)
    Befitting my ancestry
    And the life that has been,
    Patiently, sitting in wait
    For me. Before me—

Before the fall—
    I knew all, even the things
    I can't recall, consciously.
    But now I see
    How we have looked
    For me, constantly—
    How even the identities
    I mistook for me
    Have been, faithfully,
    Guiding me to now—

Overwhelmingly

Pressing me forward
Towards a semblance
Of a life lived

(Finally!)

In rapturous remembrance
Of me.

CLAIM

It became clear
    I was not the same,
    Early. I had curly hair,
    Like my island forebears'
    Heads, but instead of
    Dark and lustrous, mine
    Was just—red—

Like a sign
    Telling everyone
    To stop—
    Compelling them
    To come stare
    And wonder where this
    Little Gringo
    Came from.

The girls would go,
    "Mira, Myra, que CUTE
    El güerito!"

Fondling and touching
My auburn curls,
The way strangers
Should never do—
Like I was Exhibit A
In a petting zoo.

But, even that was better
Than the *"Ay, Foo"*
My skin and hair
Grew into—

A different *(darker)*
Stare, daring me
To glare back,
And prompt the
"Whatchoo looking at?"
That devalued
My bloodline—

Reduced
To being viewed
Through the paradigm
Of *"what eses"*
And disdainful *"dudes"*—
Rewriting my past
Into fighting cues.

I was
Racist if you do
And damned if I didn't
Defend my right to exist
In the same space
As the faces
I grew up with. This

Was my day to day—
A litany of insults
And *"que gueys"*
Fated to get the same
Results:

I hated myself.

The skin I was in
    Was too light
    To fit right,
    And I was
    Too lonely
    (Being the only
    White one)
    To fight back against
    The lack of conviction
    In my inner voice.

I heard it say,
    With Chicano diction,
    "No te dejes, guey!"

But I was
    A walking contradiction—
    And half of me
    Knew I had to stay
    Silent.

I spent years like this—
    Swinging tears
    And fists
    Against the injustice
    Of birth that placed me
    In this

Particular part of Earth—

Where my face
    And hair
    Was all the evidence
    Needed to override
    My confidence—
    My mental health—
    My essence.

But my sense of self
    Has expanded
    To include the other parts
    Handed to me—even ones
    Previously excluded
    By the easy bigotry
    Of my childhood
    History.

My neighborhood
    Has grown to embrace
    All the places
    I am from—
    Allowing me the space
    To claim my name
    The same way
    I fought
    Against the second guesses
    Of mis raíces
    En el barrio.

Now I know
    This is a different game—
    Choosing to love
    Those ignorant foos

In my head
(*Inciting misery!*)
Without losing
All the other
Parts of me.

Instead of explaining
Myself—
Chaining myself
To poorly parsed
Snippets of Spanglish memories—
I am owning these
Aspects neglected
By past me's—
Seizing power back from
The skin the world sees.

My lack of melanin
Does not change
What's within
My cachanilla soul—

The facts
That make me
A *whole* person
To be reckoned with,
Remain intact:

My skin is white.
My hair was red—
I grew up brown
Diciendo *"tu"*
And *"usted"*—
I am frijoles, tortillas
Corridos and banda,

But come from
A long line of
Mayo and white bread—

Taino and Celtic,
    Picadillo and salsa—
    Germanic Hispanic,
    Gabacho and half spic—
    Tostones, guayaba,
    Meatloaf and fish sticks—
    Menudo, sofrito,
    Cilantro and garlic.

I am who I am,
    Your tastes, notwithstanding—
    And I just might be
    Beyond your understanding.

But if I must add up
    My truth—here's the sum:

I *fought* to be me—
    And I won.

MASKS & MIRRORS

"The privilege of a lifetime is to become conscious of oneself."
— Carl Jung

The faces we fashion for the world—and the reflections we fight to recognize as our own.

IDENTIFY

How to describe
    The What of me?
    The Who and How
    And Where of me?

These words are used—
    The ones available
    To choose from.
    All slightly confused—
    Damaged *(broken, even)*
    From having been
    Spoken too frequently—
    Casually—carelessly—
    And *(sometimes)* maliciously.

I am partly some of them,
    But not completely any.
    No wonder, then,
    Though the options seem many,
    They all leave

Some of me

Out. Of everything
    I could say to explain
    Myself, I find
    Nothing purpose-built,
    Ready made or easily applied
    Towards telling you
    About the me I am

Inside. I have tried
    And failed
    Too many times to try
    Again. The When—
    The Why of me—
    The brutal, honest
    Lie of me, therefore,
    Sits quietly

Un-memorialized—
    Collecting substance
    And gravity beneath
    The fear I will always be

Unrecognized.

SELFIE

It is too easy
    For us to change
    The way we look,
    Superficially. We see
    Ourselves immediately,
    Unhappily adjusting
    Angles, filters and lighting—
    Righting the wrongs
    We perceive in the outcomes.

This is how we deceive ourselves
    To become more
    Of what we wish we were,
    And less than
    What we actually are—
    Raising the bar on reality
    Until it is too far up
    To clear without fear
    Of losing perspective
    On what is true,

And right. The objective
    Should never be
    To see and be seen
    In a light generated,
    Artificially. Yet, we venerate
    The many who can,
    Flawlessly, edit out
    The double chin,
    And splotchy skin—
    Enhancing their without
    Without fixing
    What's within.

And, so, we begin
    To disappear. We cease
    To hear the things
    That matter most—
    Preferring the empty right
    To boast about likes
    And shares.

We care
    More for the praises
    Of strangers—carelessly
    Gifted to images
    That have drifted
    Dangerously far from
    The place where our faces
    Don't have to be perfect—
    Than we do for our values
    And self-respect.

But I see you—
    Resplendent in your defects
    And impurities—your beauty

Independent of enhancement
Or false symmetry

And, I know it can be done
Differently—we can be
Better, honestly.

MIXED METAPHORS

When mixing metaphors,
    Every door is a day
    At the beach—
    Every star can be reached
    With a ray of sunshine,
    Some fishing line
    And a wishing well
    Full of church bells
    Ringing like fish in a bucket.

Fuck it.

Scramble your symbols
    And slaughter your similes—
    Grass on a prairie
    Blowing in the mountains
    Like a fountain of youth.

I don't like it—

But the truth is:
    No one gives a shit

What I think.

FLIGHT REFLEX

You are in my space—
    Your face too close to see
    Without making my intentions
    Obvious. I want to know
    Who you are, and why
    The sky has made you bold enough
    To hold your arm so close to mine.

This is not fine.
    We are not friends.
    The ends to which we travel
    Do not justify unraveling
    The social fabric that keeps

Me

Separate from

You.

And still you persist!
    As if unable to resist the desire
    To encroach on the higher place
    I have staked out here

In coach.

I do not recoil from this
    Implied intimacy,
    But do not presume
    This a sign of my complacency.

I suffer your touch
    In protest—and
    Lest you miss the real point:

This is my fucking armrest.

GENERALLY SPEAKING

I have come
    To the realization,
    It's the people
    Who make generalizations
    Who tend to feel
    Some kind of way—
    Vibrantly negative
    Sensations—
    When people stray
    Into their space
    And make
    Blanket declarations
    About their reality.

The irony
    Of me generalizing
    About generalizing
    Is not lost
    On me, but you see?
    At least I see that—

How even I can be
A caricature of self
Awareness.

This is not me
Granting myself
A pass to make light
Of statements
Lit by gas.
This is us—
Relying too heavily
On *"trust me"*
As proof of
Tricky concepts—
When empires rise,
Fall and reset
On waves of empirical
Evidence.

When sense
Is not common—
But we gave our
Two cents at the office
Of opinion—
And, so, think ourselves
Sage, when we still
Are minion—
Minding our P's and Q's
Like we're better than
All the other letters
We choose not to use—

We lose ourselves
To hubris.

This convenient seat
    In the saddle
    On a high horse
    Has addled
    The course of history
    More times than
    We can count,
    But we keep drowning
    Ourselves in founts
    Of dubious knowledge—
    Like college degrees

(Or influencers we see)

Can float us
    From the murky depths
    Of the quirky how-tos
    And FAQs
    We're submerged in.

We have converged on this point
    Of ignorance—

Convinced our identities
    Are tied to the stances
    We take—because
    A fake *"they"* is easier
    To say than a real *"we"*—
    And *"me"* is an idea
    We really have
    No grip on.

So, we slip
    On our words—
    Defending factual inaccuracies

And confirmation biases,
While all the while
These real truths
Stagnate and atrophy—
Disused and demonized
By lazy, ugly thoughts
Painted monochromatically
Because we only
Like one color.

We have stripped
The vibrancy from life
And creativity—
Shipped the work
Of self overseas
So we can feel free
To trade authenticity
For generalities.

We can still seize
This day—

But it will not be free.
The piper has come,
Gone and marched
Our innocence away.
And now

(And I say this, generally)

We have to pay.

NEGATIVE SPACE

I find myself
    Lost in this composition—
    A still life
    Of jumbled thoughts
    In constant
    Juxtaposition
    With each other.

In another life,
    I was an artist,
    Painting this collection
    Of recollections
    With minor skill and major will—
    Pushing the boundaries
    Of color and hue
    To do beautiful things
    With any subject matter
    I was faced with—

Bowls of fruit and vases

Scattered,
Then replaced
With a new set
Of objects placed
In careful arrangements.

In pursuit of perfection,
    I spent years
    Learning lighting
    And pigment,
    Fighting perspective
    And figments
    Of imagination
    To create
    My subjective view
    Of stationary objects.

In retrospect,
    I was a tyro,
    Focusing too much
    On shadow
    And shading—
    Creating what was,
    By painting what was not.

Negative space
    Was necessary,

They taught me.
    But look
    Where that got me.

A portrait of progress
    Framed
    By carefully crafted

Accents and darkness
Competing for light
And attention,
Without
Even an honorable mention
In the history of art.

I must start
Drawing differently—
Honoring
This gnawing sense
Of me clawing
Itself from the depths
Of me. There is more
To see than
What's missing.

All this time
Spent reminiscing on
Trauma and sadness
Was not wasted.
But I have tasted gladness,
Too—and it is
Madness to think
My past is nothing
But the shadows it cast.

I have amassed
Hope and laughter—
Hoarded happiness
For some (*nameless*)
Day to come after
All my cynicism
Was spent.

But darkness
    Is relentless.
    Criticisms
    And second guesses
    Abound. So, if I am
    To turn the page
    And let my true self

Take center stage,

I must relax
    This focus on
    Off center things
    And bring *joy*
    To the central place
    In this whitespace.

This life is mine—
    And I will always find
    The contrast in my past
    For present peace—

But, at the very least
    I can right *(replace!)*
    My tortured lack
    Of light, and trace
    A better outline.

THE RIME OF THE AGING
WHITE BELT

"I wish I'd started sooner,"
    I think—three or four
    Rolls a day—especially
    When I see the way
    The more advanced belts
    Own the mat. It'll be years
    Before I move like that,

If ever—I'm closer to old
    Than I am to young
    And dogs like me *(I'm told)*
    Don't mix with new tricks,
    Like take down defenses
    And ankle picks. So, maybe
    I should stick to a gentler
    Art—but this *is*
    The gentle art, they say—

Gentle the way that life is,

Maybe. I should have
A black belt in that.

(*Don't laugh!*) I've been showing
Up in this gym for forty-two years—
Went from *"Awww look at him!*
Trying kimuras from inside guard"
To flying arm bars in no time.
Thought I was a prodigy.
Dared everyone to look at me
Sideways. I could handle it,
I thought, till life started
Taking my shit—and my people.

Feels like you make one mistake
(*Or thirty?*) and fate
Takes your back and sinks
That choke in—a little dirty—
Hand over your mouth—
Nose pinched shut—
So you have no choice
But to give up
Your neck. I guess

Life twisted me—strangled me—
And, when I finally tried
To untangle me—went looking
For a little piece of me
To grow from
This humility—I found myself

Here. On this mat

I am the old guy. Master Two

White Belt—an oxymoronic way
To say I know nothing
And took my time learning it.

But I live for this.

I would rather fall apart
    Than miss a day. I swear
    I wear every bruise
    And black eye with pride
    Because *this* is the side
    Of me I want to grow old on—
    The one that's been beat to hell,
    But keeps a hold on youth—choking age
    With a cross-lapel grip
    I'm learning to use
    But still haven't mastered.

I am a white-belted
    Old bastard—

But I wear this beautiful rag
    Around my waist
    Like a white flag that says
    "Fuck you! I DON'T surrender!"
    Life didn't hand me all of that
    Gentle, tender bullshit—
    But I didn't quit!

Then I get on the ground
    Around people who are stronger—
    Better than me.
    And I let myself be
    Ignorant. Old. Weak. Scared,

Sometimes—definitely
Scarred. Then, I think

"I wish I'd started sooner"
But I get over it—

Cause it's never too late to learn
You don't know shit.

SUBJECTIVE OBJECTIVE

It would be a lie
    To say I do not
    Wish my words
    To, someday, be heard
    By many. Understood
    And digested—
    Meanings tested
    By multiple opinions and
    Perspectives.
    But that is not

My objective.

I would rather write
    In obscurity
    And say things that are
    True to me—
    Untainted by pressure
    To please,

Consistently.

I have enough
    Of that already,
    So any heady thrill
    From drinking
    The swill of recognition
    From strangers
    Is offset—
    Beset by dangers
    To my integrity—
    The potential demise
    Of the authenticity
    That makes my lines
    A balm

For me.

It would be a lie
    To say I do not
    Wish my words
    To, someday, be heard
    And understood by many—
    But, truthfully,
    That frightens me.

So I will continue
    To place each word
    And space carefully—

As if
    The only audience
    That matters is me—

And we can all pretend
    That none of this will end,

Badly.

INVISIBILITY

I am not seen.
   I mean, *really*
   Seen. I have been
   Heard—smelt—felt—
   Congratulated
   On the hand dealt me
   By fate and genes—
   Granted preferred status
   In all the ways
   We think matter
   To us—

I say *"us,"*
   But I mean *"you"*
   Not *"we"*
   And, certainly,
   Not *"me."*

Because, you see,
   I am alone

In this perspective—
This, entirely subjective,
Point of view
On who I am—
What I should be—
And what it will take
To break free
Of all this
Mental mayhem.

Some will say
This self pity is a stratagem—
A means to an end
Where all's well—
Where I have sympathy,
And attention,
And all have bent to my will
And given succor
To my demons.

But, even if it were so,
(Which it isn't)
I would still be
Alone in this
Loneliness—
This homeliness
Of will and spirit—
This unholiness
Of an existence
Whose strength and weakness
Both hinge on its persistence.

You see what I am
To you—but not to me.
And I will never be

Free of either identity.

I am trapped.

And the truth of me
    Will always be

(*Adamantly!*)

Invisible.

NO ROOM FOR QUIET

"In the end, we will not remember the words of our enemies, but the silence of our friends."
    — Martin Luther King Jr.

S ilence was never an option.

IT MATTERS

I am not black—

So I don't stress,
    Or feel like I should
    Look back at a cop,
    When I reach for my license.

I am not black—

So I take
    The things people say
    At face value—
    Because I don't worry
    About the place
    The color of my face
    Holds in their heart—
    Or their hate.

I am not black.

I do not have to discern—
    In a life or death instant—
    If my fate will rest on survival
    Lessons I have learned
    From history.
    From yesterday.
    From *every* day.

I am not black.

When *I* put my hands up
    It is not a threat—
    So it is easy
    (So easy!)
    To forget people's judgment
    Is impaired when they're scared,
    And that some of my friends—
    My family—
    Are deemed inherently scarier

Because they are black—

And driving—
    And walking—
    And talking to strangers
    About cigarettes and CDs.
    I do not see these dangers—
    Feel these dangers—
    Fear these dangers—
    Because *I* have never had to
    Hear the way the things
    Some people say
    Are laced with messages
    Traced back to a bygone day
    That is not, at all, enough gone

(*Or gone enough, at all*)
To be ignored or forgotten.

I am not black.

And if you aren't either,
Don't tell me it's nothing
To make *yourself* feel better.
I don't care if you don't understand—
Or about canned answers
(*The many who are good
Versus the few who are not*)—
Because my nephew,

Who *is* black,

Is growing up in a world
Where his truth has nothing to do
With me or my experiences,

Because I am not. Black

Is the difference
In too many *"mistakes"*—
In too many breaks from the norm,
For it to be ignored without peril.

The anger felt
Is not some feral reaction
Unhinged from fact—
So if you are not black
Don't talk to me about hypocrisy,
Because all I hear
Is you saying *"Uppity"*—
And I am *done* with that

Part of history.

I am not black—

But I am angry.
    I am tired
    Of being heartbroken
    By all the ignorant,
    Hateful things spoken
    By people *(who should know*
    They don't know better)
    In defense of indefensible actions
    Some of us are privileged
    Enough to be able to ignore.

But, for me? No more!
    Today is still too much
    Like yesterday, and if we say
    Nothing—
    And do nothing—
    We will never see
    The day where I don't have to be
    Grateful

That I am not black.

NET WORTH

We measure our worth
    In zeroes. Our heroes
    Have treasure and gold,
    And we hold these
    Truths to be
    Self evident—

Like dollars and cents
    Trump common sense—
    Like morals are worth less
    Than constructed value—

Too caught up
    In games we were taught
    To believe in before
    We were bought
    By a system that serves Them—

A bargain some struck
    With the luck of the draw

That saw them be born with
A spoon in their mouth
Made with a different metal—

Or a different mettle
That keeps them from
Settling for less
Than the houses—the cars—
While we stash pennies
In jars—far from affording
The dream they sell us.

The lies they tell us
Have us bemoaning
The fate that befell us
To keep us from things
We have learned
To believe are earned,
Not given or inherent.

We inherit the earth—
But only if our births
Give us wealth,
Or we take what we want
Through skill or stealth—
Sacrifice our health for money
We don't even hold
In our hands.

So we stand in this cycle,
Surrounded by figments
Of someone else's imagination—
Failing to understand
Our indoctrination
Into existential worthlessness—

Collecting debt
And hopelessness—
Cashing in our happiness
To get closer
To misery.

But we are more
  Than bank accounts, black cards
  And back doors to parties
  We paid to attend—more than
  The zeroes we spend—
  More than the means
  We justify to reach the end
  They *teach* us
  To chase. These base desires
  Tire out our souls.

Those goals we set
  To get what's *theirs*,
  Make us less
  Than the whole picture
  Of what existence
  Can be—make us see
  Subsistence as success—
  And yoke us
  To the apple cart
  We are meant to
  Upend. We send up

Smoke signals,
  Like advertisements
  For distress
  We were sent to shill
  By a mindset
  That cares *nothing*

For our fates,
But still berates us
For failure to comply.

But I have had enough.

I *have* enough
    Stuff to last a lifetime,
    And can no longer
    Shorten my lifeline
    To gain what is already mine:

Happiness—health—
    The infinite wealth
    Of love and friendship.

I have chased brass rings,
    Hoping they'd bring me
    One more rung up
    The proverbial ladder—
    And found myself
    Getting sadder.

Madder.

So I would rather
    Build *myself*,
    Not my roll—
    Be free to be a whole
    Me—free to receive
    The bounty of
    My spiritual evolution—
    Preemptively,
    Grant absolution
    To the internal revolution

Roiling my status quo—
Summing my worth
With different zeroes:

Zero respect for your game.
Zero respect on your name.
Zero concern
For your good luck
Or fast bucks.

Zero fucks.

"I CAN'T BREATHE"

I can't breathe.

The fact this is wrong
    Should be clear
    To me
    To you
    To anyone who
    Has eyes
    Has ears
    A heart
    A brain

I can't breathe!

There is no air here
    For your privileged view
    On what and
    Who has value

Of *course* all lives matter

But *that* is not the issue now

It's how some lives
    Black lives
    Seem to matter *less*

When there is no breath
    In their chest
    And there's a man with a gun
    And a bulletproof vest
    Holding them down
    On the ground
    Like *they're* the threat

I can't breathe

And it's not even me
    Who has to be let
    Up from this place
    Where my *face*
    Can be used as a case
    For my death
    Where my breath
    Is cut off in a way
    That would not be okay
    For the rest of us

I am not the best of us
    And maybe neither was he
    But why can't you see
    When the knee's in the back
    Face pressed
    To the black of the asphalt
    You can't debate fault
    Deflect blame

And play games with a victim's history?

I can't breathe!

It's insane how hard
    We try to lie
    To ourselves
    To each other
    To pretend
    This was not
    Someone's friend
    Brother
    Father
    Mother
    Sister
    Lover
    Daughter
    Son
    Undone in the end
    By a forever *trend* of violence

And you want SILENCE?

I can't breathe!

Still you want to argue
    With me
    Because I want to see
    People free to feel safe
    And protected
    In places and moments
    Where others expect it?

But now that this truth
    Is no longer neglected

I can no longer give you
The space to be casually racist
On the basis of what
You choose not to see

You are wrong
And your ignorance angers me

And I can't breathe.

POISON POINSETTIA

And did you sleep with her
    Asked the fat cop tasked with taking
    My complaint at the North LA Station

The answer was no
    But I felt the taint of
    Shame like he'd asked me
    About masturbation in church
    And not the woman who had been
    Stalking me for months
    With dirty talking voicemails and texts
    From always different numbers

Awkward disgusting
    Sexts I found in WhatSapp
    And today a poinsettia she left
    On my doorstep before I chased
    Her off down the street
    Yelling names I would never
    Call any woman that hadn't

Been my housekeeper

Trusted with a key
    And a view to the side of me
    That sometimes leaves
    His underwear lying by the bed
    Or piles his clean laundry on chairs
    Instead of folding it
    The privately messy man
    Who makes mistakes

Like being nice
    To a short Venezuelan lady
    Who'd been recommended to me
    By a friend who was right
    About how well she cleaned
    But didn't know in the end
    She would fall crazy for me

Talking about Jesus
    While she dusted
    The Bible on my table
    An unstable perv printing profile pics
    Of me off my socials
    And lining them up on her mantle
    And posting pics of that display on her page
    Until the day she flew into a rage
    Because I had a photo
    Of me and another woman in my house

And I fired her
    Regretted I hired her
    Through hundreds of hang up phone calls
    And every time
    I found her standing on the corner

Of my street feet shuffling
Side to side while she cried
And lied about how she only wanted
To be friends again

She was no threat to me
    I thought
    But I bought security cameras
    For my house anyway
    Cause somehow I knew one day
    She'd get to me
    And I'd be sorry if I didn't
    See her coming

And still my dogs saw her first
    Barking at her though the window
    By the door while she left
    That fucking plant on my porch
    Like Christmas made things good
    With me and she hadn't torched my
    Trust in rules and boundaries

So yeah I snapped and chased her
    But what could I do really
    All one hundred-eighty pounds of me
    Yelling obscenities at a five foot nothing
    Monster who had sapped me
    Of my peace for months

So I just screamed
    I'm calling the police

A promise made suddenly hollow
    By the obese officer who couldn't be
    Bothered to take a report

Until I said if she attacked me
I wanted a record to protect

My word against hers

So he sighed and I started my story
He smirked and asked
And did you sleep with her
Like he was looking to blame me

Shame me

And it worked cuz
I felt like a *"real man"*
Would've handled it

No wonder women don't report this shit.

SHELTER IN PLACE

They said they heard
    Firecrackers—
    Like Fourth of July
    In November.

Remember
    Those paper balls
    Of gunpowder we threw
    Against classroom walls?
    Like that.

Firecrackers—

Familiar like New Year's
    And childhood.

They heard
    Firecrackers.
    And then, some of them

Never heard anything

Again.

I.C.E.

Some words flow
    Out of me
    Smoothly—

Drip—
    Bling
    On the tip of my tongue

Songs sung
    Soothing souls
    And hearts—

Some words
    Are a whole
    Other thing entirely

They start off
    As rocks
    Lumps of coal

Compacted
    And changed
    By fire

We hide and hold
    But do not
    Control

We touch them
    And feel cold
    We throw them

And are told
    We are
    Inciting riot

Disturbing the quiet
    Peace of complacency
    And compliance

We speak
    In defiance
    And are considered armed

And dangerous—
    Power feels harmed
    And violently turns

On us—
    Our speech
    Is distrusted

Sharp and hard
    Diamond encrusted
    Projectiles

And shards
    Made lethal
    By truth

And solidarity
    We are
    Disgusted

By what we see—
    By the lack
    Of humanity

Running free
    In our streets
    Masks and badges

Doubling as
    White sheets
    Bodies dragged

And handcuffed
    At the feet
    Of oppression

While they make light
    Of our skin—
    Our kin

Our aggression
    Is the logical progression
    Of this

Regression to a
    State of repression—
    Macro-expressions

Of racist disdain
    Their words do little
    To explain away

Headlines concocted
    To limit the backtalk
    The rage—

But we will do more
    Than turn this page—
    We will *burn* this page

This chapter—
    This book
    Of lies about values

The system tries
    To pass off
    As justice

When really
    It's just this—
    Cowardly vigilantes

Masquerading
    As law and order
    That require our *disorder*

Civil or uncivil
    Until this thing is done—
    Until this fight is won

They claim to be right
    Wing—patriotism
    Taking flight

But we already
  Have words for this
  Fascism—Racism

We will wield them
  Again and again
  Boulders thrown down

From our bastions
  Of black and brown
  To land square

On the shoulders
  Of those who dare
  To assail us

These words are rough
  And uncut but
  They will not fail us

Against these
  Costume quality
  Cubic zirconia

Without distinction
  Only a stone's throw
  Away from extinction

Lashing out
  In the final spasms
  Of supposed supremacy

Before being swallowed
  By the yawning chasm
  Of history—

Some words
    Flow out of me
    Violently

But when else
    Are we supposed
    To use them

When the day
    Is ruled by bigotry
    And hate

What else should we say
    Answer fast
    Or melt away—

We will *not* wait.

CALAVERAS

When the skeletons
    In our closets get bold—
    When the old restrictions
    Of fear and shame
    Lose their hold,
    And release those vile bones
    Into the streets,

What do we do?

How do we defeat
    The things said aloud—
    Previously crowded, silently,
    Into our heads—that now
    Spill into the light?

How do we fight

The fears that lead
    To hate? How do we

Suffocate these thoughts
And actions, when they are
So clearly refractions—
Reflections of ideas
We should have
Obliterated long ago?

We are armed and ready
With deflections—
Bullet-point-proof
Vests on our chests,
And masks to hide
Our true faces.

We are practiced at deception—
Harboring our own
Preconceptions—
While our demons displace
People with theirs.

Some of us care enough
To wave our feeble signs—
Chanting
"Fight the power"
And praying
It will stave off
These abominations
Of opinion and strength—
Without recanting
The lengths we go
To keep our own
Amalgamations
Of fear and ignorance
Private.

But we have let
    These secret skeletons
    Escape, now.
    Doesn't matter how,
    Or why, or what kind of
    Lies we've told ourselves
    About whether or not

They exist.

They subsist on our hate—
    Exaggerated expressions
    Of manufactured nightmares
    We feed in our sleep—
    That we keep alive
    In our minds—
    That we find ways
    To justify
    With our experiences—
    Our memories—
    Our all too corruptible
    Senses of self.

These bones are ours—
    Frames on which
    To hang our
    Haunted hatred
    And putrid desires.
    They cannot be
    Simply tamped down.
    They must be stamped on
    And trampled—
    Bones shattered,
    Stacked and fired
    In funeral pyres of protest

And liberation from
The expectations we've carried
About how this nation
Can come by
Peace, peacefully.

We have made this.
And the only way
We right this,
Is to fight this.

A NOTE TO THE PHILISTINES

I am not weak—
    So, when I speak, I don't expect
    My words to be neglected
    Lightly. If I am, rightly, angry
    At what I see, underestimate me
    At your peril.

This spine of mine
    Was designed to stand up
    Straight—against hate—
    Against the fear that, of late,
    Has been swung like a weapon,
    Blindly. So, when I talk—
    Mind me.

I recognize (*amidst the lies*
    Of the subjective—told to further
    Old objectives—echoes
    Of our own perspectives),
    My words—though considered

And reconsidered, carefully—
Are merely minor harmony
To all the choruses we trumpet—
To all the anger we let loose
Into the world around us.

But I am not static.

I move
With the times that surround us.
I have a voice
And, armed with the right to use it,
Still sling my sounds against the temples
Of giants who would see me lose it.

You can ignore me—
But if you really knew
What my words can do—
You would fear me.

And you will hear me.

MAPS FOR THE NEXT WORLD

❧

"Caminante, no hay camino, se hace camino al andar."
(Traveler, there is no road; you make the road by walking.)
— Antonio Machado

*M*ovement, maturity, and the quiet wisdom that guides us to higher places. The journey doesn't end—it shifts.

UNSHRUNK

I wanted to be
    Six feet tall. A dream
    Easily expected for a boy,
    Born small in stature,
    To want his height to match
    The might of his intellect.

My body neglected to comply, though,
    So I resigned myself
    To five-foot-nine, and
    A lifetime of short jokes—
    Fun poked at my expense
    By people with more height
    Than intelligence—
    Or even common sense.

And, though it would seem
    My towering IQ
    Should do nicely as
    Recompense for not getting

To shop at Big and Tall,
My antagonists insisted
I keep those bigger parts
Of me small, as well—
Lest I make them insecure
About *their* lack
Of mental stature.

And I played along,
    Confining my potential
    Within a deferential hell
    Of mediocrity *(for me)*—
    Which still smacked
    Of superiority *(to them)*—
    So even my forced atrophy
    Was not enough
    For me to be accepted by people
    I had to stoop to see
    Eye to eye with.

I did enough—said enough
    To get by
    Without drawing undue
    Attention—to avoid
    The appearance of condescension
    And remain welcome
    In my communities—

Diminished but permitted—
    So long as I limited
    The amount
    Of *(perceived)* intellectual
    Crimes I committed
    Against their relative
    Stupidity.

No one has ever reciprocated
    My misguided generosity
    By apologizing to me
    For being taller.

I have made myself
    Smaller to save their egos—
    Foregone millions
    Of raised hands
    And *"I knows"*—
    Distorted myself—
    Contorted myself
    To seem I was unable
    To reach mental shelves
    They couldn't
    Jump and touch
    To *save* themselves—
    And all I have to show
    For myself
    Is bad psychological posture.

I am *(most likely)*
    Smarter than you.
    But I have also
    Worked harder than you
    To ensure my brain
    Didn't cause you pain
    By comparison.

And I am done
    With such idiocy.

I want to be
    All of me—
    So all you might

Recall of me
Is the sound
Of the *(rusty?)*
Mental double clutch
That leaves you
In the dust of me—

The way you feel
About that
Is no longer
My responsibility.

ONE WISE THING

This may be the one wise thing I ever write.
    Therefore, I must not
    Be careless of where I write it.
    Though wiser men may waste their wisdom
    In number one best sellers
    And bathroom stalls,
    I must be more frugal with mine.

Do I bank it here
    On a private page and hope
    It will collect interest
    Someday? Do I part with wisdom
    In prose, or have the audacity
    To share sagacity
    In poetry? Must I say it
    Well, or can I write it quickly—
    Badly? You might say,

This being my only chance at being
    Genius, I should not be

So flippant with it—
But having very little wisdom,
I would not take you seriously.

Still, having not yet written my one wise thing,
I am a wise man still.
And wise men keep their thoughts quiet
Long enough to think themselves wise
Another day.

So, being in no hurry to be dumb,
I will wait to be wise.

This may be the one wise thing I will ever write.

THE GRASS IS GREENER

The lawn in my backyard
    Started dying in July—
    The dry summer drying
    The green blades of spring
    Until, absent the respite
    Only rain can bring,
    They began to desiccate.

By late August, there was
    Little left of the lush landscape
    But sparsely spaced patches,
    Barely scraping by.
    And, by September,
    There was nothing
    By which to remember
    What had been before—
    Just an eyesore brought about
    By drought and neglect.

In the midst of this hell,

October leaves fell on ground
Hardened to everything
(*But unwanted clumps of clover*),
Blowing in brown and orange bunches
Through November until,
By December,

It was over.

It was never supposed to be here, though,
  This greenery—just artificial scenery
  To liven the view
  Through my French doors.
  Nothing more
  Than a product of my imagination,
  Which, without irrigation,
  Simply ceased to exist.

Then (*if you can believe this?*)
  It began to rain.

At first, I watched
  Through panes of glass
  As the sky spattered
  The earth with drops
  Of life that mattered little,
  And thought this
  Smattering of water just fleeting
  Hope, unheeded.

But it persisted
  (*This record shattering precipitation*)
  Until the lawn, seeded in promise
  Long gone—which had only existed
  By force of will and folly—

Began to, slowly, grow again,
Through dampened dirt and hesitation.

And still it rained—

Sustained and heavy downpours—
    Like a levee in the heavens
    Had broken.

Through weeks I watched
    (*Behind those doors*),
    Wondering how much more
    Of this my world could take—
    Finding it impossible
    There could be any thirst
    Left to slake—
    Thinking God must have
    (*Mistakenly*) sent me
    Someone else's weather.

But, whether or not
    That was true,
    When the sun finally
    Did break through the clouded sky,
    That grass which I had
    (*Through despair and necessity*)
    Left to die untended,
    Miraculously ended its decline
    To complete its re-emergence.

Now I sit in this resurgence,
    Doors flung open
    To the possibility
    This could be a new existence—
    That life sprung forward

From pain *(and all this rain!)*
Can be full and green
And lushly lived—
That joy and dreams
That seemed dead can, instead,
Do more than just survive—

That I can
  (Say it!)
  Thrive.

BE

I flit about
From thought to thought,
Like the bees I see
Buzzing from lavender
To myrtle tree—
Hurtling industriously
Towards lemon blossoms.

We are awesomely active
(The bees and me),
Ceaselessly gathering
Pollen and perspective
From flower and thought,

Respectively. Mental inactivity
Is as foreign to me
As a day off would be
To a worker bee.
Busy is the norm for me—
And today,

I am true to form.

But, I am starting
    To see a different way—
    A means to stay longer
    In each second—
    To ignore the next place
    That beckons me—

To be
    A less frantic me,
    Needlessly hurrying
    Between everything
    That worries me
    And, instead,
    Resting
    (Ill-advisedly?)
    On laurels—and bowers
    Of flowers I have
    Already drunk

From. This inactivity
    Comes unnaturally—
    But I feel how
    This mind grind
    Constantly saps me
    Of joy from things
    That would otherwise
    Be beautiful—

Trees—Flowers—The birds
    (And these goddamn bees!)

Reminding me
    The whole fucking reason

For being alive
Isn't the day to day
Fight and flight—

It's the way
Each moment sits
On my senses—
Patiently pollinating
My memory
With beauty and mystery.

I do not yet know
The answer to happiness—
But I don't think
It's busyness.

And an increasingly bigger
Part of me
Believes that (*maybe*)
If I can just be more

Still,

It will come to me.

THE GRAY IN MY BEARD

I love the way
    The gray is growing in
    My beard. My whole life
    I feared getting old—

Told myself I'd be lucky
    If I did—because
    It seemed easier
    To imagine never aging
    Than to do the work
    Of engaging with the idea
    I might be living
    Life, for years.

But, these fears are fading
    (Along with the melanin
    In the hair on my face)
    With time—with every line
    The world has placed

In my skin. I am better
At seeing the beauty
In my wrinkles—

The way my laughs crinkle
The edges of my eyes—

The way my body
Still tries to keep up
With my mind's drive—

The way these changes
Remind me
I am still alive.

I love the gray
In my beard. It speaks
Of wisdom (*some earned*
And some left
To be learned) and the man
I have—and can still—
Become. I must,

Sometimes, will myself
From one day to the next,
But the gray tells the story
Of how many days
I have done that,
Successfully—

How the young and old
In me can blend together,
Gracefully—

How the me I see

(With this graying beard)
Is so much better—
So much more—
Than I always feared
I would be.

LOCATION

I don't know where this is—
    This place where there is
    A perpetual smile
    On my face. This joy
    Is somewhat foreign
    To me—a destination
    I could, previously, never
    Begin to go to
    Without hesitation—

Without reservation—

I still cannot be here
    With no fear, but I feel
    (*If not safe*)
    Stable in my trepidation.
    And that is enough.

I don't know what this is.
    But i do *not* miss

What it was before—

Broken

Promises—forgotten
    Hopes and doors closed
    To possibility. It seems to me

This is something new,
    And the best thing
    To do is to be
    In it—to sit with this
    Beauty, unexplained—

To be unrestrained
    In my joy and acceptance
    Of the fact
    I am happy

Here—

With this.

I have questions
    And doubts and fears,
    But I am willing
    To concede
    I don't need answers,
    Yet—to forget

I have been hurt
    And confused and scared—
    That I have felt used
    And neglected—disrespected
    And lied to. This place—

This thing—

It brings me happiness.

And I want nothing to do
    With anything that keeps
    Me away from it—
    From *you*.

So, I will stay
    Here with this—

So I don't miss anything
    Precious
    In this *(strange?)* land.
    I don't need to understand
    Where or what
    This is,
    Or where it will go.

It feels good
    Just to know—
    I love
    Where I am

Now.

MEETING HAPPINESS

The first thing I noticed
    Was sunshine seeping
    Into my veins—like nature,
    Slowly creeping over walls
    And walkways—erasing
    Pathways paved with habits
    And familiarity—
    Gently swallowing patterns
    (So intently created!)
    Until all my thoughts
    Dissipated
    Beneath the relaxing
    Onslaught of happiness.

I was at once
    Less, but so much more—
    As if, by shutting the door
    On my pain
    And private pettiness—
    By thinking less—I could be more

Sane. More me.

Suddenly, there was just love
    And bliss, and this
    Easiness—
    No judgment. No shame.
    No blame game
    To play.

I never knew
    This way existed—

That joy could be
    So insistent—
    So persistently present
    It could bully my barriers
    Into irrelevance.

It was *decadent*.

Like sunshine and flowers
    And the heady scents
    Of springs and summers—
    Like beaches and forests
    Growing next to flowing streams
    And sparkling lakes—
    All the places I have neglected
    To take more time to rest in.

But I am here

Now. Aware and awake,
    And in no hurry
    To avoid being
    Buried beneath this moment

Of peace and warm intent.

I am meant to be
    Happier—
    Healthier—
    Closer to where
    I am now
    Than to where I've been—

That place is fading fast
    Behind me.

I am here

Now. Come find me.

ABRACADABRA

It is said
    The First Word
    Spoke itself.

Not written—
    Not read
    By some ancient sage
    From a page
    In a book on a shelf
    Containing the world's
    Wealth of knowledge—
    But self conjured
    Into existence
    Despite the resistance
    Of Nothing.

Darkness

Then

Light—

Sparked from will
    Growing
    To, eventually, fill
    The stillness
    Of this void
    Where nothing was
    Before.
    Power deployed
    From, into, and through
    The endless
    Vacuum.

I presume
    This to be true.

Me, who
    Speaks nothing—
    Writes nothing—
    Lights nothing
    With my empty phrases,
    Then grieves
    The empty phases
    Of the harvest moon—
    Who leaves
    Dreams unplanted—
    Hope supplanted
    Too soon by
    Fear.

I hear the word
    Spoken
    And, immediately,
    See the cost

Incurred by being
Brought to life—
Calculating loss
And strife until
My miraculous present
Is rife with debt
Due to the future.

My words are wounds,
    Sutured together
    With syntax and grammar—
    Nails tethered to
    The hammer of my thoughts,
    Dragged along
    And caught in a constant
    Cycle of construction
    And destruction.

But the First Word
    Spoke itself—

With all the voice
    And agency
    I fear
    Some cosmic choice
    Divorced from me,
    It simply *was*
    And came to be.

And then it grew,
    Untamed and free,
    Into the sounds
    Surrounding me—
    Into the mystic
    Mystery

Of who
I am
And what I see—

Into the words
I twist and twirl
And tame and train
And sic on me.

Their pattern
Is ingrained on me,
And I have (*mostly*),
Willingly,
Tuned into
Their frequency
To limit my capacity
For life and wealth
And love and health—

But the First Word
Spoke itself—

When there was
None before—
No fear, no pain,
No poor mental health—
No judgment, disdain,
Regrets
And no shame
To provide the environ
For guilt to subsist—

Just a radical sound—
And a will
To exist.

And so I persist
    In freeing my tongue
    From chaos and rot—
    Cleaving to life,
    Not the words
    That came after—
    To escape from the strife—
    To write a new chapter
    With wholeness of hope
    And abundance
    Of laughter.

Reality
    Is me,
    And *must* be
    What I seek—
    If I can let go and

Simply—Speak.

FULL VOICE

We all have agency.
    We all have choice—

But some things
    Can only be said
    With the right voice.

Instead of being
    Heard clearly,
    Messages
    Can be muddled
    And lost
    When tossed from
    Lesser tongues—
    Undone by timbre
    And diction—

But *you* have
    No such restriction.

This is no question
    Of volume—no knob
    To turn high enough
    To earn you attention.
    It's a function
    Of *identity*—the one
    Which, when set free,
    Can be a beacon
    Of laughter and hope
    And beauty.

It's not a song,
    A note, a riff—

It is

A gift.

HERE

I am still
   Here

I have been
   Lost

Here

But I am not
   Anymore

I am just
   Here

Where I am

And
   I don't need
   To be

DAVID ANDREW TITTLE

Anywhere else

THANK YOU

"Nosotros, los de entonces, ya no somos los mismos."
 — Pablo Neruda,

*W*hen next we meet, we will be different—even in the ways we have remained the same. So, I thank you for sharing this unique moment of your existence with the echoes of mine.

WE MADE SOMETHING GOOD.

—DAVID ANDREW TITTLE

ACKNOWLEDGMENTS

Thanks to all who have been a part of my conscious collective consciousness for this poem:

- Leena—for being a consistent inspiration, audience, and partner in spiritual growth.
- My sister, Lisa—my original "fan" and most honest critic.
- My brothers, Benji and Daniel—for, lovingly, ensuring language never gets lazy or boring.
- My parents, Ken and Diana—for their generosity of love and trauma, and the ways that shaped the art of me.
- The entire cast of characters from Calexico, Yale, LA and beyond—if you don't know who you are, then you're probably not reading this book.
- Special thanks to Anze Ban Virant - ABV atelier design—for his beautiful and inspired cover art.

ABOUT THE AUTHOR

David Andrew Tittle is a multicultural poet and writer, born and
   raised on the US/Mexico border in Calexico, California.
   His work blends sharp social commentary with wit and moments
   of raw tenderness, exploring identity, resistance, grief, and moral
   clarity.

A Yale alum, he lives and writes in Los Angeles.

www.ingramcontent.com/pod-product-compliance
Lightning Source LLC
Chambersburg PA
CBHW071218090426
42736CB00014B/2876